How to Get Him Back

I Miss My Ex-Boyfriend and Now I Want Him Back

by Nick Kirkpatrick

Table of Contents

Introduction

Relationships can, and do, recycle from time to time. The process of getting back together with an ex-boyfriend however, is a very delicate and often labor-intensive endeavor. Pursuing an ex presents us with unique challenges that we need to be aware of if we want to have a chance at success.

As you probably know, there's no way to force someone to love you or want you. If that were the case, love wouldn't be meaningful. It wouldn't have its mystique. There would be nothing special or unique about it, nothing worth coveting, nothing worth obsessing over. If love were a simple commodity, we wouldn't send out a distress beacon to Google and scour the internet for advice, support, and solutions. No one can dominate or dictate the tides of romance, not even the most beautiful, the fabulously wealthy, the immensely powerful, the famous, or the strong. We are all vulnerable to heartbreak. Like death, love is "the great equalizer."

If you're fully committed to getting back together with your ex-boyfriend, it's going to take some work. This is not going to happen overnight and if it does happen overnight, it's probably not going to last. This book is for women who are interested in building a healthy and lasting relationship with a strong foundation to build upon for years to come. It's not for women who want to pursue on-again off-again, emotionally unfulfilling and stomach-turning romance. Quick and easy reconciliations with your ex-boyfriend, often born out of loneliness and/or alcohol are a recipe for exacerbated emotional pain, resentment, and insecurity. If you want to get your ex back permanently and build a life of happiness together, then you need to read this book from start to finish.

A few things this book is not:

- A promise of a magic or guaranteed result.

- A half-baked serving of tired advice and cliché.

- A catalog of manipulative mind games aimed at inducing jealousy or making your ex think you're someone you're not.

What this book is:

- A coaching guide that will help you understand and commit to the work involved in repairing a wounded relationship.

- A practical, step-by-step, real-world approach to re-establishing a romantic relationship with your ex-boyfriend and becoming attractive in his eyes again.

- A book that's written on the premise that you want to be back together with your ex-boyfriend and that you're not interested in pursuing other men at the moment.

What you'll gain by reading this book and following its directions is the best possible chance to get your ex-boyfriend back. If you're ready to roll up your sleeves and get started, then read on.

Chapter 1: Figure Out Exactly What You Want

Do this. Just do it. Write down the characteristics of your ideal man. And see if you can do this without describing your ex to a T. You want him back. Fine. But for the sake of this exercise, pretend you already have him back. Pretend he's head over heels in love with you. Pretend that the two of you are living your life together, happy as can be. And, as with any relationship, you face challenges. You have to learn to compromise with one another. But because you love him so much, you can make these compromises. You can accept him for the wonderful man that he is. You overlook his bad habits, because you love him. You may even quietly adore your ex-boyfriend's quirks, faults, and short-comings. That's fine. That's called being in love, but this exercise isn't about who you love. In this exercise you've been happily married already for many years and you understand the realities of marriage and how life is challenging *with anyone*. And you've decided to take some personal time to wax romantic and envision "the perfect man."

This exercise is about indulging in a personal vision. A fantasy. After all, no one is perfect— not you, not your best friend, not your father or mother, not your ex-boyfriend. So write down on a piece of paper the attributes you think make up "the perfect man." This exercise is about *you*, and no one else. Don't think too much about how this specifically relates to your quest to get back together with "him." Just do the exercise and see what happens.

If you're having trouble separating yourself from your current emotional state and doing this exercise with a clear head, then imagine you're six years old again and you've just seen Snow White for the first time. Start with your basic vision of "Prince Charming." What makes him so perfect? Now, hold that vision, but envision yourself growing older with it. Now your 16. What does Prince Charming look like now? What does he look like when you're 21? What will he look like when you're 60?

Some Things to Consider:

Is there a particular look you like in a man, a hair style, skin tone, build, do you like a certain fashion sense?

Do you like men who are funny, smart, sexy, caring, all of the above? Write it all out.

Do you want your ideal man to have a certain career? Feel free to get specific here. Maybe he's a lawyer or a doctor, an actor or a musician. What career would nicely complement or support your own career ambitions. What type of profession would you like to learn more about and discuss the daily activities of over the dinner table each night?

Does your ideal man like certain types of TV shows, movies, music, games?

Is your ideal man the strong and silent type, reserved during the day, and thoughtfully pensive and quiet at night, though still manly? Or is he the affectionate romantic type who can't keep his hands off of you?

Does your ideal man want to take you out a lot or is he more of a home body?

(If at any time you find yourself drifting into describing your ex-boyfriend, that's fine. Quietly and without judgment on yourself acknowledge that the person you have feelings for – your ex – is leaking into the person you're trying to imagine in this particular exercise). It's tough, but if getting your ex back, is what you really want, you need to focus and do this exercise properly.

Take at least 30 minutes to do this exercise. Write down as much as you can about this "ideal mate" character, and remember to preserve your character's unique identity. Your ex-boyfriend is human, and therefore flawed. You can be in love with your ex-boyfriend. You can't be in love with the person you come up with in this exercise, because as far as you know, he only exists in your imagination.

You may be wondering why you're doing this exercise. You already know who you want, your ex, duh.

Well, if you're going to have any chance at getting your ex back, you're going to have to rediscover and reassert a certain reality. And that reality is this: there was a time in your life when you did not know your ex, and at some point during this time you were able to sustain yourself emotionally. You were "ok." In order to get your ex-boyfriend back, you're going to need to get back in touch with that reality. You are you. You always have been you and you always will be you. If you get your ex-boyfriend back, you'll still be you. If you do not get your ex-boyfriend back, you'll still be you. There's nothing you can do that will change the fact that you are you.

The fact that you were once without your ex and you were ok, is not going to be an easy headspace to rediscover. Sure you know it's the truth. You've not always been heartbroken and pining for "him." This is the reality of your past, sure, but using that reality to inform your present mindset and sensibility is extremely difficult. Understanding the reality of self is very much a transcendental task, almost poetic, romantic and epic in its own way, for it is, ironically, crucial to you should you have any chance at getting back together with your ex-boyfriend. Understanding that you are you and always will be you won't blot out your emotional pain, but it can help you envision a simple road map that will show you how to live your life without worrying about your ex boyfriend.

Often what happens in breakups — when your self-esteem is low and you are emotionally wounded — is that your personal identity gets caught up in the "identity of the relationship." The relationship becomes an entity in its own right, its own self in a way, and you feel that somewhere buried within that "self" of the relationship is "you." Which, of course, is simply not practically or empirically accurate. If you were to reestablish your relationship with your ex-boyfriend, you would still have personal experiences, personal trials, personal problems that you and you alone would have to deal with. You would not be immune from personal unhappiness or hardship. Even in the happiest of relationships, there are still challenges. A good relationship will provide you with support and love, but even the best relationships will never relieve you of the burden of being an individual self. The burden of self is that you must support and love *you*.

Self-love is an extremely important power, because if you have it, no one can take it away from you. Self-love is the fundamental attribute of an emotionally healthy and emotionally empowered person. Without it, you will be limited severely in your personal and professional pursuits. And as for getting your ex-boyfriend back, without self-love you've got no chance in hell.

Do you have the attributes of your ideal man written down on paper? Great! Now you know that even when it comes to romance and relationships, you are still your own person. There's no escaping this reality. Now let's move on to the next phase.

Chapter 2: Go On a Date Without a Date

You're not going to feel like doing this, but you need to do it anyway. Go out on a date with yourself. Tell your friends you're busy. Go do a little shopping, or go see a movie. Take a walk on the beach, or go bowling, or go to a museum. Go to a bar, or out to dinner if you're particularly brave. Maybe you live in a smaller town and you don't want anyone to see you out all by yourself. If that's the case, drive yourself to the nearest big city, or go to the next town over, or go somewhere where you're sure you won't run into anyone you know, or go a yoga lesson or a seminar. It's important that you do this so shut down all the excuses you'll find not to do it. This is about spending quality time with someone who matters, you!

You really do owe it to yourself to get out, but if you insist on staying in, make yourself a nice dinner. Try a new recipe. Dress up a bit and look nice. It sounds strange, but do it regardless. After dinner and desert, treat yourself to a good movie.

Your solitary date may indeed feel haunted by loneliness and you're not going to be able to stop thinking about "him," and that's totally normal. It's ok. That's to be expected. You're going to have thoughts of your ex being there with you and you're going to wonder what he's doing. And you're going to be replaying conversations the two of you had and wondering if you had acted a bit differently or said something a bit differently, if things would have turned out better. You know, the same stuff you normally indulge in during your regular day to day. Recognize these thoughts as normal, natural, but not based in the current reality. You're out by yourself for the evening and that's all there is to it. It doesn't matter what anyone else is doing.

After you get through your first "self-date," repeating the routine should get easier. Try to go out on a "date" at least once a week, and especially when you "don't feel like doing it." Every time you push yourself to do something in this program that you "don't feel like doing," you're getting yourself closer to your ultimate goal of becoming that confident, independent person that your ex will find irresistible!

Chapter 3: Self Reinvention

It's much easier for a relationship to be repaired if the people getting back together aren't really the same people who broke up. You have a better chance at getting back together with your ex-boyfriend if you do a little transformative work during your single time.

You can begin with simple and superficial changes: try a new hairstyle or go get your hair cut, take up a new hobby like yoga or kick boxing, change up your daily routine by taking a different route to work or trying different types of food. Meanwhile, try and stay focused on you for now.

Don't go out of your way to advertise to your ex (or anyone) all the cool, new, and interesting things you're up to. So you get up at 6am and complete a grinding hour of Pilates. Great. Don't seek recognition from your ex (or anyone). Have faith and be patient. If you're doing good *for* yourself, *by* yourself, you *will* realize a payoff. It's that simple. Keep up a new healthy hobby for just two weeks and you're bound to immediately start looking and feeling better.

Self-reinvention is important because it will help you push the reset button on the emotional dynamics between you and your ex boyfriend. When people break up, they do so for a reason, it's often something quite subtle and ineffable, which is why people who are unsuccessful with getting back together with their exes are apt to go through so many failed attempts, make-ups after break-ups after make-ups, on-again, off-again and so on. Because they think that by identifying the problem at a rational level – I need to be more patient in the relationship, or I need to control my anger better in the relationship, or I need to be more affectionate in the relationship – they can at once repair the emotional defects of the relationship as well. That's simply not the case. There's only one way to repair emotional fall out from a breakup, through time and self-work. And this emotional repair is what's required if a broken relationship is going to have a chance at ever being healed in a manner that's sustainable and healthy. Patience, thus becomes incredibly important, even vital factor in getting back your ex. More on the importance of patience in the following chapter.

Chapter 4: Don't Blow It!

You've probably been reading this book and wondering why there's been nothing discussed about how to talk to your ex-boyfriend and reengage him in your life. There are only two things you need to know regarding the subject of contacting your ex.

1) You would not be reading this book if the breakup with your ex-boyfriend did not leave you profoundly wounded and distraught.

2) Any contact you have with your ex while in this current state of vulnerability and distress will only contaminate your recovery process. It will do no good for your own personal well-being, and it will obliterate your prospects of getting back together with your ex in any sort of long-term arrangement.

And sure, if you follow the advice in this book, you will frequently have moments where you "feel well" and you think "Gee, I don't feel emotionally distressed at this particular time, maybe this is the perfect opportunity to reach out to my ex and tell him how much I want him back, or show him how well I'm doing."

Don't do this! If you're feeling well, it's probably because you've been following the advice in this book. So don't stop now! In the following, final chapters, we'll talk about when it's ok to make contact with your ex.

Chapter 5: The Golden Rule of Getting Back Together

Most women who attempt to get back together with their ex boyfriends fail. They fail because they are impatient and they attempt to force the situation by initiating contact with their ex long before the appropriate time. You can avoid this stumbling block by learning "The Golden Rule of Getting Back Together" with your ex boyfriend.

Don't Contact Your Ex Before You Are Ready to Face the Reality That the Two of You Will Never Be Together Again.

Don't worry, I don't mean to say that you actually won't be back together again. But what I'm suggesting is that you need to be in a calm enough state of mind, and strong enough emotionally, that the idea of never getting back together again doesn't upset you.

There's no way to tell one way or another whether someone wants you back unless you ask them, but if someone ended a relationship with you, then you can assume that it's because they don't want to be in a relationship with you, and they may not change their mind on that for some time.

27

When you reveal to your ex that you want to get back together with him, you're leaving yourself incredibly vulnerable, and it's best not to risk bringing more pain and rejection on yourself if you're not yet strong enough to accept and absorb the emotional impact. So don't. Stay put for a while, not in a manipulative "I'm going to make him wonder about me" sort of way, but in a level headed, highly aware, self-directed sort of way. Don't concern yourself at all with what's in his head. You can't control that. All you control is you.

If you follow the instructions in this book— continuing to pursue positive self-reinvention and making time to spend with You—then you will eventually cultivate a strong sense of self that did exist, does exist, and will exist completely outside of the relationship with your ex. Repairing a relationship in a meaningful way is not possible if both of the parties are not whole as individuals. If the parties are acting out of neediness or desperation, then the relationship is doomed to fail again and again.

As for timeliness (i.e.: how long after the breakup do you tell your ex that you miss him and would like to be together again as a couple?), the answer is that it doesn't really matter all that much. As soon as you're ready to permanently accept the possibility that you will never ever be together again with your ex-boyfriend, then you are ready to contact him. If you still have a longing of such extreme intensity that you can't imagine your life without this person, then you need to stay away. Focus on yourself, remember the reality that you were you before the relationship and you were ok, and let things develop slowly and naturally in your life.

Don't look for reasons to contact your ex. Don't tell yourself you're ready if deep down you know you're not. In fact, the longer you wait the better the overall chances you will have of getting back together in a healthy, sustainable fashion. That's difficult advice to swallow when you're hurting but's it's the best advice available. There's nothing wrong with having feelings for someone that aren't requited. Take as much time as you need.

Conclusion

When we become involved with another human being on an intimate emotional level, we give away parts our "self." We also give away certain securities and privacies. For some reason, it's very difficult to manipulate an ex-lover who doesn't have feelings for you. If you truly care about this person, you will instinctively resist the urge to be underhanded and play mind games. You will want to believe that this is someone to whom you can simply bare your soul to and he will accept you for who you are. The intense need to hold those whom we have feelings for in such high esteem makes us vulnerable. What if the object of our love is no longer willing to extend to us that unconditional acceptance?

In a lot of ways, dealing with a break up and doing all you can to salvage some hope of real reconciliation is merely the process of personal vulnerability management. If your emotions are raw, be conscious of that fact. Try and see yourself through an objective and removed lens and assess your emotional vulnerability. Use a 1 to 10 scale with 10 being extremely vulnerable and heart broken. Now, commit to yourself that you will at least wait until you are consistently at a 5 before attempting something as stressful as reaching out to your ex boyfriend for reconciliation.

It's also a good idea to listen to the opinions of your friends about when and how you should go about getting your ex back. If your friends have experienced their own share of difficulties in relationships then they will be well positioned to give you advice. If they advise giving yourself more time to regroup, take them seriously. It's ok to be vulnerable, don't try and act secure and strong. Your ex knows you and will be able to read your emotions and when your inauthenticity shines through, it won't be very attractive.

Being attractive to your ex or anyone else comes from maintaining and exhibiting a strong center of self. Knowing this and acting accordingly is going to be critical to your quest to get your ex back. Stay focused and trust the advice of your friends and this book. Don't trust the advice of your emotions and fantasies. Work hard to better yourself and be comfortable with your own company and before long, if it's meant to be, your ex will come back around again. And you'll be ready.

Finally, I'd like to thank you for purchasing this book! If you found it helpful, I'd greatly appreciate it if you'd take a moment to leave a review on Amazon. Thank you!

Printed in Great Britain .
by Amazon

68448763R00031